I LIKE TO BE QUIET

by Joni Caldwell

Illustrated by
Jon Bonjour

I Like To Be Quiet
by Joni Caldwell

Illustrated by Jon Bonjour

Text & illustration copyright © 2020 Joni Caldwell

CAUTION: All rights reserved. No part of this publication may be reproduced, stored in a retrieval system, or transmitted in any form or by any means electronic, mechanical, photocopy, recording, or other, except for brief quotations in written reviews, without the prior written permission of the publisher.

Published in 2020 by:
Climbing Angel Publishing
PO Box 32381, Knoxville, Tennessee 37930
www.ClimbingAngel.com

First Edition December 2020
Printed in the United States of America
Cover design by Jon Bonjour
Interior design by Climbing Angel Publishing

ISBN: 978-1-64921-788-2

For Alyson, my very own quiet child.

I Like To Be Quiet

I am Jamie.

I like to be quiet.

Sometimes I wish I was just like my big sister, Anna.

She is great!

Anna can talk and talk and talk all day.

I don't know how she can think of so many things to say!!!

…but I like to watch Anna talk

and think about what I will say

when it is my turn.

Sometimes I wish I was just like my dad.
He is outgoing and kind.
He can talk to anybody,
 even if he doesn't know them.

He likes to help people and always knows
how to make them feel good…

One day there was a new girl on the bus.
She was sitting all by herself
                and she looked a little sad.

I sat down beside her.

We didn't say anything to each other,
but when I smiled at her, she smiled back,
and she didn't look sad anymore.

Sometimes I wish I was just like
my little brother Jonathan.

He tells the funniest stories and makes everyone

laugh and **laugh** and **laugh**...

… but I like to be quiet.

One day, when it was just me and Jonathan,
I told him a story I made up,
and it made *HIM* laugh!

And then we both laughed SO HARD!

Sometimes I wish I was just like my mom.
She always knows what to do
because she keeps a list.

Every morning and every night,
she helps us to remember what to do next…

…but I like to be quiet.

Sometimes I make a list,
but it's not for the whole family.

Just like Anna,

I say something when I *want* to,

but I take some time to think about

what I will say first.

Just like my dad, I am kind,
and I want to make other people feel good,

but I don't feel comfortable
talking to people I don't know yet.

Just like Jonathan,
I can tell a funny story,

but I don't do it
in front of everybody.

Just like my mom,
	I like to know what comes next,
and sometimes I make a list too…

but my list is
		just for me and Jonathan.

I guess I am a little like my loud and funny family…
but I'm glad that I am a little different, too.

I like to be quiet, and my family loves me
just the way I am.

THE END

ABOUT CLIMBING ANGEL PUBLISHING

Climbing Angel Publishing exists for the purpose of sharing stories of hope and encouragement, aiding in the gathering together of community, and supporting the process of betterment. The following books are available at ClimbingAngel.com and major bookstores.

ADULT BOOKS: *(Romans 8:28-30)*

In His Image, Sam Polson (English, Romanian, & Mandarin)
By Faith, Sam Polson (English & Romanian)
My Birthday Gift to Jesus, Lisa Soland
Without Ceasing, Dr. Dennis Davidson
SonLight: Daily Light from the Pages of God's Word, Sam Polson
Corona Victus: Conquering the Virus of Fear, Sam Polson
Art Bushing: His Diary, Letters, & Photographs of WWII, Art Bushing
Art & Dotty: His Diary, Their Letters & Photographs of WWII, Art Bushing
Trimisul, Stan Johnson (available in Romanian only)
Life Changing Prayer, Sam Polson

CHILDREN'S BOOKS: *(Philippians 4:8)*

The Christmas Tree Angel, Lisa Soland
The Unmade Moose, Lisa Soland
Thump, Lisa Soland
Somebunny To Love, Lisa Soland (English & Mandarin)
The Truth about God's Rainbow, Lisa Soland
God's Promises, Lisa Soland
The Boy & The Bagel Necklace, Lisa Soland
God's Hands and Feet, Lisa Soland
I Like To Be Quiet, Joni Caldwell
Wheels Off!, Karlie Saumier

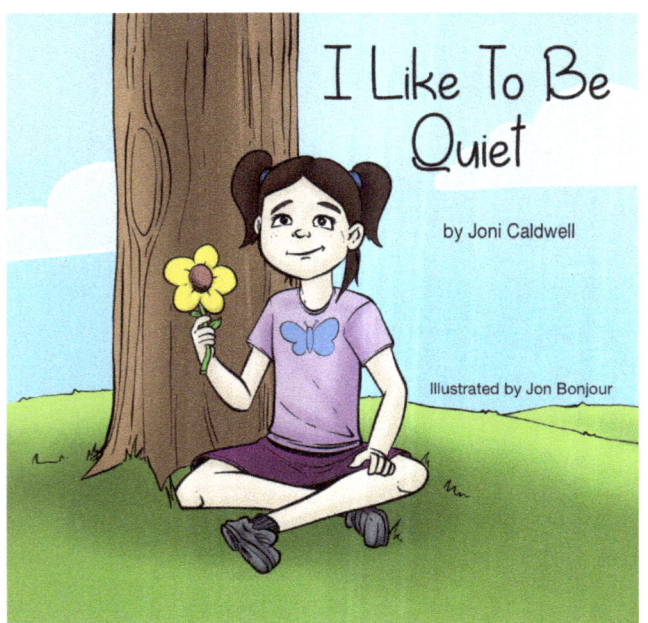

I LIKE TO BE QUIET
by Joni Caldwell

This book is written to honor *the quiet child*, the child that likes to observe, the child that enjoys a little alone time to think. Like me, I know you are amazed as you watch your quiet child. I hope this book will serve as the backdrop for you to snuggle into each other for a while. Let's make sure they know how interesting they are and how very proud we are of them, *just the way they are.*

GOD'S HANDS & FEET
by Lisa Soland

In *God's Hands & Feet*, Fred's mother teaches him invaluable lessons on how to be "one of God's very important ambassadors." She explains, "You are to be God's hands and feet because when God wants to do something good in this world, He sometimes uses us to do it."

"Start children off on the way they should go, and even when they are old they will not turn from it." (Proverbs 22:6 NIV)

THE BOY & THE BAGEL NECKLACE
by Lisa Soland

In *The Boy and the Bagel Necklace*, Andrew, a resident of a Romanian orphanage, tells us the story of when Jesus visited him in a dream. Jesus tells Andrew not to worry, that everything is going to be all right. Soon after, the leadership in Romania changes and little Andrew is adopted and brought to America where he learns that Jesus Christ is more than just a nice man who visits desperate children in their dreams. When little Andrew learns just how much God loves him, his life is radically changed.

WHEELS OFF!
by Karlie Saumier

Wheels Off! is Hazel and Henry's first of many adventures together. Henry is Hazel's little brother, who sometimes wishes he wasn't so little. While playing at the local playground, a group of bullies pick on Henry, but his sister is there to help him discover that "Heaven on Earth" is not that far away.

"A terrific Christ-inspired story of forgiveness, family, and friendship."
– Lisa Soland, author